COLLEGE RETREAT WITH HURRICANE KATRINA

BY
AARON JOSEPH MOORE STOVALL

"I Owe My Life to the Lord!!"

Bloomington, IN  Milton Keynes, UK

AuthorHouse™
1663 Liberty Drive, Suite 200
Bloomington, IN 47403
www.authorhouse.com
Phone: 1-800-839-8640

AuthorHouse™ UK Ltd.
500 Avebury Boulevard
Central Milton Keynes, MK9 2BE
www.authorhouse.co.uk
Phone: 08001974150

First published by AuthorHouse 3/9/2006

ISBN: 1-4259-1378-4 (sc)

*Printed in the United States of America
Bloomington, Indiana*

This book is printed on acid-free paper.

DEDICATION

I dedicate this journal to: My friends at Xavier University---Jamar, Chris, Brandon, and Jonathan for keeping me in motion when we were venturing through this catastrophic event; to my family and all the special friends that prayed for my rescue and were willing to listen to my story once I returned home; and finally to all the people living in New Orleans, and to their families and friends everywhere.

What the enemy meant for evil God will turn it around for good God bless!

ACKNOWLEDGMENTS

Thanks to the staff at Southern Louisiana University & Xavier University of Louisiana; all the police officers in New Orleans; and all the volunteers and resident directors who stayed with us through the hurricane.

Special thanks to my parents, Drs. Arthur & Joyce Stovall, Brother Artis Stovall, Grandmother Ida Moore, Uncle Joseph S. Moore (Pete) & his wife Aunt Cynthia, Mayor Martin O'Malley of Baltimore, and Oblate Sister Mary Emily Burks of Baltimore. Pastor Steve Houpe and First Lady Mrs. Donna Leah Houpe and Harvest Church of Kansas City, Missouri for prayers.

Special thanks to Cousins Chris and Ronald Stovall, Uncle Willie Stovall & wife Aunt Mary, Uncle Henry Stovall & Aunt Lorna, Cousin Melodie

Stovall, Uncle Tyrone Rhames & wife Aunt Doris, Aunt Patricia Watson, Judge Henry Green & wife Mrs. Shirley, Mr. Leo Sam, Aunt Pam Robinson, Ms Beverly Jackson, Mrs. Chris Norris & daughter Lindsey, Dr. & Mrs. Dalenberg, Ms Bernice Thomas, Mrs. Joanna, Mrs. Donna Freelon & daughter Shannon, Brandon Stephens, Jemarcus Best, Curtis Marks, Leonard Parker, Veronica Johnson, Gina, Canieta Creighton, Ebony Hardon, Shamier Bouie, Sara Rimmerman, Tiesha Stewart, Selena Burns, Brittney Belford, Brittney Stovall, Brittney Allison, LaToi-ya Jackson, Kasey Webb, Michael Adams, Gary Lange and Shannon Hoins. I appreciate your prayers and support more than you will ever know.

I am very grateful to Ms Joyce Williams, Mrs. Cynthia Moore, Mrs. Dorothy Ross Mckenny for editorial assistance; and to Mr. Richard Fulcher for assistance with the graphic design.

Above all, I thank God!

TABLE OF CONTENTS

DAY 1: Saturday, August 27, 2005
Terrifying knocks on my dorm room door

9: 00 A.M. There were three terrifying booming knocks that hit my room door in St. Micheal's Dormitory at Xavier University in Louisiana. I woke up completely frantic! I answered the door and asked, "What's going on?" "There's a hurricane coming to New Orleans tomorrow night so you must pack your belongings and leave," said the RD (resident director).

The first thing that came to my mind was that I had very little money available on hand, and that I could probably "tough" out this hurricane. Besides, last summer while participating in Xavier University's summer camp, there was a hurricane warning, so I moved off campus to a hotel in New Orleans, but there were only strong winds and heavy raining for several hours. I thought nothing serious was going to happen this time either. I decided to sit back and watch everyone else panic.

9:50 A.M. "Oh my gosh!" "We're all going to die!" said Chris, a homeboy from Louisiana, in a rather sarcastic manner. "No we're not," said Jamar. Jamar was my roommate from California. He was the calm one in the group. "The most that will probably happen is some strong winds and a little rain; I'm not used to this stuff in California," said Jamar. "I want to go home," said Chris in a joking manner. As I looked around the room, I noticed that not everyone was taking this hurricane seriously, and I certainly wasn't taking it seriously. I decided to take a nap to escape the madness for a few hours.

1:00 P.M. "Wake up Aaron, look at everyone who's leaving!" said Chris. "Are you serious?" I said. Now imagine everyone being over zealous, just for the mere fact that we thought school would be closed for at least one week. As I saw more and more people leaving, I thought, "I don't want to be here alone no matter what happens."

3:00 P.M. "Let's look for places to stay," said Chris. We began to think of places to go. We definitely didn't want to be the only ones left in the dorm. I searched everywhere in Baton Rouge, Louisiana, and every hotel was full. Then we began to worry about the situation. To add to the dilemma, all the Greyhound Stations were either closed or full. That's when panic began to set in just a little. But I still refused to fly back home to Kansas, because I didn't know when classes would resume, and I certainly did not want to get behind in my studies. In addition, I didn't want my parent's money spent flying me to and from Kansas for a false hurricane alarm.

5:00 P.M. "Hey Aaron, Jamar, and Chris, dinner is being served," said Jonathan a friend from California and a very comical character. Even though it looked as if we were staying in the dorms throughout the hurricane, no one panicked and everyone was surprisingly calm. While eating dinner, more and more people were telling me where they were going, and that they were not staying in New Orleans at any cost. All I kept thinking was, "They're really just wasting their money, because nothing is going to happen." Absolutely nothing is going to happen.

9:00 P.M. For the rest of the night, Jamar, Chris and I decided to relax and watch television.

In Saint Michael's dorm, there were nineteen male students who had decided to stay, and I felt pretty secure about my decision to stay. I felt confident that if the hurricane hit, it really wouldn't affect me. All I could think about at this point was, "Only time will tell."

<u>DAY 2: Sunday, August 28, 2005</u>
Goodbye to the girls

11:00 A.M. "It looks pretty normal to me," I said. I didn't realize that hurricane Katrina was going to strike later that night. That morning I was really drowsy, and I wasn't in the mood to participate in any physical activities including walking. So I stayed in bed the entire morning.

3:00 P.M. "Aaron---let's say goodbye to the girls," said Chris. When I heard him say "girls"--- my adrenalin started pumping and momentarily I perked up. But the girls were leaving to go back to the girls' dorm and we would no longer be kept together. The news that the girls were leaving to return to their dorm made me feel down again. Chris and I went downstairs to say goodbye, and this time there was one thing different I noticed about the girls that greatly concerned me. I could see they were showing signs of fear. My intuition told me that women are more perceptive than men about these sorts of things. At this point, I became greatly concerned about the hurricane, but I knew there was nothing I could do but pray. When I returned back to the dorm, I was told that the students who had not left the campus were stuck in the dorms for the long haul, because the city of New Orleans was shut down.

5:00 P.M. "It's dinner time Aaron," said Jamar. We all went to eat dinner in the cafeteria for the last time as a group of young men and women. Even the cafeteria workers at Xavier had quit working to evacuate the city. To see the cafeteria empty without the hustle and bustle of the students was scary, and I knew without a doubt that most of the students had also left the campus. This was a reality check, which was humbling and a little frightening. "Reality check, you can say that again!"

7:00 P.M. I received a telephone call from my mother and Uncle Pete from Baltimore, Maryland. My mother had attended her family reunion in Maryland on Saturday, August 27th, and Uncle Pete was driving her to Baltimore so that she could fly out of Baltimore Washington International (BWI) Airport to return to Kansas the next day. When talking to me about the hurricane situation, I detected from my mother's voice her deep concern for me still being in the dorm at Xavier University. I told her to pray. Then she passed the telephone to Uncle Pete. Uncle Pete is a detective for the Mayor of Baltimore. He started asking me questions as to why I was still there, and told me that I should leave New Orleans if it was at all possible. He thoroughly briefed me on what to expect when the hurricane came. I could feel my uncle's sincere concern for my welfare. While this made me feel a whole lot better, I felt even more vulnerable. Uncle Pete had been in the detective business for more than twenty years, and I knew that he knew what he was talking about.

9:00 P.M. "Aaron we're going to the girls' dorm!" said Brandon, my observant friend from Maryland. Most of the girls had left the campus, but there were a few who had stayed. Going to the dorm to stay with the girls was quite exciting to me. Imagine going on a free two night vacation...this was going to be fun, we thought. We were playing music, dancing, and packing, all at the same time. I tried not to get too excited, but I did make sure to pack my required cosmetics such as a toothbrush, toothpaste, mouthwash, soap, deodorant, cologne, and a hairbrush.

10:00 P.M. "What's your name?" said Veronica, a vivacious young lady from Houston, Texas. "I'm Aaron." "Where are you from?" I said. "I am from Houston," she said. As she and I kept talking, I knew she was going to be one of my close friends. While talking to her, I noticed that I began to forget about hurricane Katrina. All I could think was, "I'm having fun again."

11:00 P.M. "Gentlemen, go to the sixth floor we're having a meeting," said the lead resident director (RD). I had an idea of what the meeting was going to be about, but I didn't know the extent of it. "Gentlemen, there will be no funny business, on any of the floors that the girls are on." "Security guards will be watching the doors and hallways, to make sure you guys don't try anything slick," said the RD. The first thing that came to my mind was, "Dang! There's a hurricane going on--worry about that, not us." But then I remembered, they had to do their job. Of course, the meeting backfired, because in college rules are made and then broken. However, for the most part we still respected the RDs' rules. That night I went straight to bed. The other guys stayed up playing cards until 4:00 A.M.

DAY 3: Monday, August 29, 2005
Hurricane Katrina from my dorm room

7:00 A.M. "Breakfast time," said the RD. When I woke up, I had the worst headache. That night we had to sleep on the wet cement floor, and I only had one cover. The floor was wet, because the ceiling was leaking from the rain of hurricane Katrina. But nothing could prepare me for what I was getting ready to see outside the windows of the sixth floor of the campus building where we were staying. I got up slowly from the floor yawning and stretching. I was walking towards the window when I saw the most amazing natural disaster in my life.

The streets were flooded; the water had risen about five feet. The wind was blowing very hard. I could see cars floating down the street in the rushing water. I could see where the wind had blown the roof off of three buildings on campus. I ran downstairs to alert my friends about what I was witnessing. When I got down to the lobby, some of the students were in shock, and the others were laughing as if to say, "I told you so!" I couldn't believe what my eyes were seeing. I have never experienced a hurricane before. I am from Leavenworth, Kansas—the tornado alley, and I have witnessed the aftermath of tornadoes, but nothing this extreme. All I kept thinking was, "How am I getting home?" I didn't want to be stuck in New Orleans for more than a week, especially if I wasn't going to college. Instantly, I became angry, very angry! Then I knew that I should have gone home or to the Superdome. However, I didn't want to go to the Superdome, because I knew the Superdome would have been overcrowded. I started justifying to myself why I didn't go home. I felt I had been stubborn about staying, because I didn't want my parents spending their money. Angry with myself, I started punching the wall. I desperately wanted to be at home. I thought, "Who knows when we will go home?" Meanwhile, the other students were either eating or sleeping. I tried to converse with the sisters, thinking that this would help to pump me up. I had to keep moving, because if I sat in one place too long, I became drowsy.

12:00 Noon "I need to check my voicemail," said Jamar. "So do I," I said. I went upstairs where we had slept to get my cell phone. When I turned on my cell phone and checked my voicemail, I realized how many people were genuinely concerned about me. I had seven messages from family members and friends. "Aaron you should have left New Orleans." "You need to come home," said Uncle Pete. "Aaron where are you?" "Call me back son," said my Mom. "Grandson, are you safe?" said my Grandma. "Aaron I saw the news." "I hope you're ok!" said Lindsay. She is one of my neighbors and best friends that lived in Leavenworth, Kansas. The more messages I heard, the more upset I became with myself. After listening to my messages, I felt slightly depressed. For the first time, I was homesick. I honestly felt drained and had no energy. I didn't feel like moving a muscle. I just sat quietly at the window and watched the storm. I listened to the wind bashing against the window pane. The wind tended to echo the pending anguish that was to come.

6:00 P.M. "Young man, go to the lobby; we're having a meeting," said the RD. This time I wasn't sure what the meeting was about. I do know one thing; the guys were not acting like angels. I will put it this way---the night the boys and girls stayed in the same dorm it turned into the 1970's Woodstock.

8:15 P.M. "Fellows get in the van we are taking you back to the men's dorm," said the RD. Right then and there, I knew this was no longer going to be fun. They took away our source of fun, which were the females. To make things worse, the van we were to ride in to get to the dorm was one-fourth emerged in water, and it was dark outside. We could barely see what was going on outside. I forgot to mention that the power went out early that morning, and we were using flashlights that day. It was pitch black in the dorms, because the RD didn't want to exhaust the life of the batteries in the flashlights.

The scenery was a replica of everyone's worst nightmare. New Orleans was flooded, and it looked like we were in one of those scary movies trapped on a lake. When we arrived back at the men's dorm, everyone went straight to bed. There was no electricity and we were depressed.

<u>DAY 4: Tuesday, August 30, 2005</u>
A victim of hurricane Katrina

10:00 A.M. "They're serving food Aaron," said Jamar. At this time, I was really not hungry. I knew I was not going to exert myself, and I felt I didn't need to eat. When I looked out of the windows, I could see the water slowly rising. I didn't know that one of the levees in New Orleans had breached, causing the water to rise. Remember, there was no electricity and we had no access to the news broadcast on television about the damage that hurricane Katrina was doing. I thought that since New Orleans was six feet under sea level that the water on the higher grounds was flowing down to New Orleans. The water had risen to six feet, up about a foot from yesterday, when it was approximately five feet. To say the least, things were not looking hopeful.

All the hot water in the shower was gone and I had to take cold showers, which I had never done before. The room had begun to smell like mildew and even the Kleenex tissues were moist because of the extreme humidity. As I was writing this journal, I could barely see what I was writing in pencil due to the humidity. I started to wonder if and when we would run out of bottled water and food. We heard on a battery operated radio that people were dying. This touched my heart in a way that it had never been touched before.

I had heard about natural disasters on television and about people dying all of the time in this nation and other countries throughout the world. Now, I was a victim of a natural disaster that they are talking about on the news. I was stunned to say the least. To top things off, my cell phone had no signal and I could not receive nor make telephone calls. I began to just sit back and reminisce on my elementary school years, my junior and senior high school days, and anything that would keep me feeling happy. Just prior to hurricane Katrina hitting New Orleans, I tried to console my Dad by telling him that I was mentally and physically ok. I can honestly say that it is getting really tough.

6:00 P.M. "Aaron, are you ok man?" said Jonathan. "Not really," I said. I began to notice that fatigue was setting in, and I had no energy to do anything. I just wanted to sleep the whole day away. As the evening passed, the guys started getting restless. This was obvious, and I believe it was because we could not communicate with the females. I also became short tempered, which was not my temperament and out of character for me. I became annoyed whenever I heard another guy's voice. Needless to say, the night had only begun.

8:00 P.M. "Aaron, it's time to be initiated," said Bob. "Initiated for what?" I said. "You'll see," he said. I was thinking, "Oh great, the whole dorm has gone crazy," but I was still somewhat curious to see what was going to happen. I go to Bob's room, and I'm standing there thinking, "What's going on in here?" There are 12 guys standing in a group looking at me like they are going to jump me. The room was pitch black with just one flashlight. Bob tells me "Put out your hand." I like an idiot put out my hand. He starts spraying my hand with hair spray, then he takes a lighter and lights my hand on fire. I shook the flame off my hand so fast that I couldn't believe it myself, nor could I believe what just happened.

I could barely breathe! Too many thoughts were bombarding my head. I immediately left the room and got alone to think. I didn't want to react out of character. I wondered why they did that--just something to do—wow.

9:00 P.M. "I `m going to bed fellows," I said. I couldn't afford to take anymore surprises that night. I laid down in my bed, but I didn't get to sleep until 2:00 A.M. I couldn't believe what had just happened to me.

Courtesy of National Medical Association News

A National Guard humvee patrolled the streets of New Orleans after Hurricane Katrina devastated the city.

Courtesy of National Medical Association News

Hurricane Katrina's floodwaters prohibited mobility throughout the city of New Orleans.

Courtesy of National Medical Association News

Hurricane Katrina caused widespread destruction in the communities of New Orleans.

DAY 5: Wednesday, August 31, 2005
No signs of being rescued

10:00 A.M. "Aaron, they're serving food downstairs," said Jamar. "Cool, I'll be down," I said. By this time, my body felt drained. I went to brush my teeth. There was no water. Therefore, I couldn't wash my face, take a shower, or flush the toilet. I thought, "What else must go wrong in order for us to get evacuated out of here?" However, there were no signs of being rescued. Every time I thought we were about to be evacuated from the dorms I would see policemen coming on boats bringing us more bottle water. I dropped my head and cringed! Not knowing when we were going to leave New Orleans made the ordeal even more laborious.

By the way, for breakfast that morning we had croissant bread and cold sliced turkey. We probably should have been more grateful since there were thousands of people stranded on the outside without food or water.

It was two days post hurricane Katrina, and I hadn't talked to my family members or friends. This greatly bothered me. I wondered how my friend Brandon, his girlfriend Ashley, and their baby son were doing. I thought about how much I missed my family and friends in Leavenworth; and I wondered if they knew this. I was definitely homesick. To make matters worse, I heard on the radio that it might take months for the water in New Orleans to recede; and there was no way to be evacuated out of the city until the water receded.

2:00 P.M. "Are you about to go back to sleep?" said Jamar. I said, "Yea." When I laid my head down on the pillow, my spirit, mind, and body were suddenly over taken by a feeling of great relaxation. I can honestly say that I hadn't felt this relaxed since the hurricane nightmare had begun. I remember dreaming about my friends back home, and in my dream I became sad. Once I awakened, I realized how sensitive I had become. I felt as though my mind over matter was beginning to grow weaker. I begin to forget how to spell small words like "the" and "about."

I thought this was happening to me because I was sleeping too much. I felt I was being held hostage by the hurricane, and I tried to sleep each day away. The more I slept the less energy I had. I had no energy to talk, and I wanted to be left alone to pray and think. I heard on the radio that three persons were raped in the Superdome; I thought, "Man, I am blessed that I didn't go there."

8:00 P.M. I prayed and thought about what was happening. I said, "I'm through thinking about tonight." "I'm going to lie down."

11:00 P.M. I could not get to sleep. The room was very hot. I felt like I was being punished. It was extremely difficult for me to sleep, because it was very hot and humid. I thought, "If only I could have taken a shower!" "A shower would have felt great in that extreme weather."

DAY 6: Thursday, September 1, 2005
"Get down! Get down!"

6:00 A.M. "Why am I even awake?" I thought. This was the second day without showering. Last night was the first night I didn't use the bathroom. Just imagine, I didn't want to eat because I didn't want to have to use the bathroom. The toilets didn't flush, because there was no water in the toilet bowls. Two days of feces had accumulated in the toilets and every toilet was nearly completely full. The bathroom smelled like a toxic waste dump and no one wanted to use it. In addition, there was a gas leak in our dorm. The terrible smell of sewage along with the toxic gas fumes permeated everywhere throughout the building. This was outrageous!

I felt that my memory was deteriorating, but I didn't feel panicky. However, I could sense that a big disaster was about to happen in the dorm if we were not evacuated soon. I thought, "What if someone twisted their ankle, got bit by a spider, had a seizure, or required medical assistance for whatever reason?" "They would be stuck!" "There was no relief in site, and no way to a hospital." Indeed, this bothered me, and I became even more frustrated!

While listening to the radio, I heard that hundreds of people were dying everyday in the Superdome. Outside of my dorm window, I could hear the resident directors arguing about social issues in the United States. I knew it was time to pray.

8:00 A.M. Wow! I couldn't believe that I'm in this nightmare. However, I must give thanks to God for everything! I knew that if I didn't leave the dorm by the next day, I was going to lose hope. I had become so good at sleeping to prevent myself from becoming depressed that I could fall asleep anytime of the day at will.

9:00 A.M. I decided that there was nothing better for me to do, but to go to sleep.

9:10 A.M. Boom! Boom! Boom! "Everyone wake up---they have boats for us outside," said one of the dorm mates. Then he said, "You can only bring one bag." I laughed hard and said, "I would be darned if they keep me from bringing all my belongings." Ironically, the same joy that was on the faces of the guys who agreed to stay was now on our faces when we were told we were leaving. I have never in my life felt happier than in that moment. I packed a few of my clothes, and two pairs of tennis shoes in my luggage. I just wanted out! Nothing else mattered at the time.

Once I got on the boat, I felt greatly relieved. The driver of the boat began to brief us about the deaths in New Orleans. They told us that they saved an eleven year old boy who watched his mother die in the storm. This was the most dreadful story that I had heard. It topped all the other bad stories that I had heard in New Orleans. To say the least, I was very upset and angry, but I didn't know at whom to direct my anger.

The rescuers took us to the highway overpass where we had to wait for buses to come and transport us out of New Orleans to the airport in Baton Rouge. Sounds simple, right? Ha, Ha, Ha--We arrived at the highway overpass, and walked up to the area of the overpass where the buses were expected to pick us up. When I got to the top of the overpass everything looked like a scene out of a scary movie when the world ended, and only a few people survived. It was out of control!

11:10 A.M. Once we got to the highway overpass, my cellular phone worked. I called my mother to tell her that we were waiting to get on the buses leaving out of New Orleans. I couldn't reach my Mom at work, so I called my brother, Artis, and told him that I was ok.

2:00 P.M. "Darn, when are these buses coming?" said Jonathan. What made the wait worst was the fact that it was raining on us, and we didn't want to risk sitting on the ground so we stood for five hours. I still can't believe I literally stood in one place for five hours. We were standing so long that my feet went numb. This had never happened to me before.

3:00 P.M. The soldiers brought us food on a helicopter. This sounds like a good thing right? Well, it almost was. The majority of the people who lived in New Orleans hadn't eaten since Monday. Let's just say they wanted food too. When the first batch of food came, it was dispersed among Xavier University students, and then the second batch of food came and it was dispersed amongst the locals. When the first batch of food came and was given to the Xavier students, the locals didn't know that a second batch of food was coming for them. They became very upset. They didn't cause any harm, but they definitely voiced their opinion about the situation. Once the people received their food, everything calmed down.

7:00 P.M. "I see buses!" said Chris. Instantly, I could feel my heart pounding so hard that I thought the girl standing next to me could hear it thumping. I looked to see how many buses were coming, and I saw only six. I noticed that the buses were not school or public transportation buses, but rather military style caravans. They could transport only eighteen to twenty persons depending on how much luggage you had. There were at least 300 people on the highway overpass waiting to be transported out of New Orleans. I became worried when I heard someone say, "If you have any large luggage leave it! You can bring one small piece of luggage." "We have to get everyone on these buses." When I heard this, I became very upset. I felt sick to my stomach, and literally wanted to vomit. I thought, "There has to be a way for me to get my luggage on the bus even though it is large." That's when I prayed and asked God to help me, and to give me favor with the policemen. God answered my prayer. More buses came, and I was able to get on the military bus with my luggage, and my backpack containing my laptop computer and books. I praised God the entire bus ride!

7:30 P.M. I thought, "This isn't the airport. Why are we getting off the bus?" Well, the military buses had carried us about a twenty minute ride from our original waiting area to another waiting area at another highway overpass. While we were waiting for the next caravan of buses to come and transport us to Southern Louisiana University (SLU) in Baton Rouge, Louisiana, up drove Reverend Jesse Jackson. It seemed as though there was a glow of light surrounding Reverend Jackson as he prayed for us. His presence and prayer was a beacon of hope. This was surreal! Yes, oh yes, "Keep Hope Alive!" "God is good!" I kept saying to myself and to others who were near to hear.

9:00 P.M. We were very happy to see the school buses! Unfortunately, this was not an uneventful transition. When the school buses were coming at night to carry us to SLU, they accidentally stopped for a group of locals, because it was dark and they thought the locals were us. Once they realized that the locals were not Xavier University students they asked them to get off the buses. The locals were very disturbed when they were told to leave the buses, because they had been without food, water and rest for three days. Many had walked several miles to this highway overpass from the Superdome and other shelters when they heard that the buses were going to pick up students here. It was total chaos, and most people wanted to leave the city of New Orleans immediately.

When we finally got on the buses, the police hurriedly briefed us and told us that we had to bend down in our seats, because there was no telling what the locals might throw or shoot at us when we drove pass them. I looked up and saw two armed policemen standing at the bus doors who were prepared to shoot locals who attempted to get on the buses, or to harm us. I slipped out of my seat, and quickly crouched down in the aisle between the seats where I sat on the floor of the bus. I thought, "This is like a scene straight out of a violent horror movie!" "This was an unreal happening and was certainly non-fiction." This was `the real deal' and I didn't want any parts of this action. When we drove by the locals the police yelled, "Get down! Get down!" I was so terrified! I could hardly breathe. Today, I have more appreciation and respect for the police officers than I have ever had before. They `had my back' that night, and I am and will always be forever grateful.

12:00 A.M. "Finally we arrived in Baton Rouge, Louisiana at SLU. Once we were in the gymnasium, a feeling of relief rushed through my body. I plugged up my cellular phone, and the first person I called was my Mom. I said, "Mom, I'm safe!" "Can you get me an airplane ticket home?" "I want to get home as soon as possible." Of course, my Mom got me an airplane ticket to Kansas that same day. I could hear her sobs of relief...along with mine.

Day 7: Friday, September 2, 2005
Wake up!

7:00 A.M. "Aaron, wake up, they're taking kids to the airport in Baton Rouge," said Veronica. I woke up happy that morning. I could care less that I hadn't taken a shower in four days. I just wanted to go home. I said farewell to my friends, especially my home girl Veronica. I climbed into the airport van. I was on my way home. Yes! Yes! Yes! Once I got to the airport in Baton Rouge, a sudden rush of emotions over took me. I broke down in the middle of the airport, and cried good solid man tears for approximately thirty seconds.

While waiting for my outbound flight, I had time to reflect on everything that I had encountered for six days as one of Hurricane Katrina's victims in New Orleans. This encounter was a devastating experience, but my encounter with God at a two day retreat at my church helped me to survive. With and through God, all things are possible; I remember hearing those words of encouragement, "Have faith and trust in the Lord and He will answer your prayers." Wow, did He answer! Today I have a different outlook on life. I had a chance to live, see and feel my faith in action by placing first my utmost trust in the Lord. I called my family and friends to let them know that I was on my way home. I almost cried amidst my burst of laughter and prayers of thanks on every single phone call. I could not hold my excitement.

Once I got on the airplane, I knew everything was ok. Looking wistfully out the window, I felt the presence of God. "You are safe, my son," a voice seemed to say. The sky seemed to me to be so very, very blue and unobtrusive, the clouds, so calm and unconcerned with the frailties of the world. With a sigh, I closed my eyes in quiet contemplation.

To be honest, I still feel very uneasy about a lot of things that happened over those terrifying days. I thank God for protecting me, and bringing me safely home. I pray for the safety of the other evacuees.

ABOUT THE AUTHOR

Aaron Joseph Moore Stovall was born on April 11, 1987, in Kansas City, Kansas. His elementary and secondary school years were spent in Leavenworth, Kansas school district. He excelled not only academically, but also involved himself with many other aspects of high school extra-curricular activities while also assuming leadership roles in the community.

As a model citizen, Aaron participated with his high school's Peer Mediation Team, a selective group of students who attempted to assist students with their many school problems and concerns while attending school. As a member of this peer team, he gave many motivational, uplifting lectures to the youth at the middle schools in the Leavenworth school district. Aaron attends church and has volunteered his service to enhancing positive community efforts.

In the fall of 2005, Aaron was offered a Xavier University of Louisiana merit-based scholarship. He was inducted into the Xavier's Howard Hughes Biomedical Honor Corps. He was offered a Dillard University Dean Scholarship for the Fall, 2005 term, a Dillard University Tennis Scholarship, and was awarded the Presidential Scholarship by Kansas City Kansas Community College.

Aaron is now attending Morehouse College in Atlanta, Georgia.